How-to Tips

How to Correct the Sentences

1. Read each sentence. Think about what it says.

2. Look for mistakes.

3. Fix the mistakes. You may need to add, change, or take out a word.

4. Rewrite each sentence neatly on the line. (Use another sheet of paper if you need more space.)

5. Reread your new sentence. Does it make sense and sound right?

How to Answer the Vocabulary Questions

1. Read the directions.

   - To choose a word: Read and think about each choice.

   - To figure out a word: Look for root words, affixes, or clues in a sentence.

2. Think about what you will do.

3. Reread and check your work. Does it make sense?

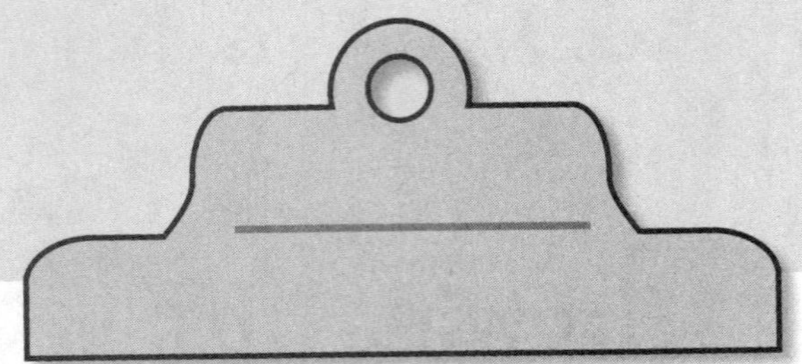

Sentence Editing Checklist

Use this checklist to help correct each sentence.

- ❑ Does the sentence begin with a capital letter?

- ❑ Does the sentence have end punctuation? (**. ? !**)

- ❑ Did I use capital letters to begin words that need them?
  Examples:
    - days (Monday)
    - months (July)
    - names of people or pets (Ben, Spot)

- ❑ Did I choose the correct word?
    - homophones (to, two, too)
    - verb forms (tell, told, will tell)
    - pronouns (he, them, that)
    - prepositions (on, above, before)
    - adjectives (red, little)

- ❑ Did I write a complete sentence?

- ❑ Did I put commas where they belong?
    - dates (May 6, 2015)
    - words in a series (We have a ball, a bat, and a mitt.)

- ❑ Did I put apostrophes where they belong?
    - contractions (don't)
    - possessives (Pat's)

Correct the sentences.

1. do you like animales

____

2. pam wants a pet dog or cat of she own

____

Circle the word that names a noun .

3. funny   puppy   running   fast

Write a question about snakes.

4. ____

Correct the sentences.

1. a pond is smallest than a lake

____

2. green plants grows in a pond

____

Circle the word that means more than one pond .

3. pondes   ponds   pond

Write the two words that are in bullfrog .

4. ______________   ______________

Correct the sentences.

1. how long did it take to ran the race

____

2. you ran so fast

____

Circle the word that is spelled correctly **.**

3. thu   dhe   the

Circle the word that means about the same as try **.**

4. You did well because of your good effort.

Correct the sentences.

1. we is going to mexico this summer

____

2. are you going to fly in an airplane or ride in a car

____

Circle the words that go together **.**

3. airplane   bike   car   map

Circle three words that can mean more than one person **.**

4. us   me   we   you

Read the word and its definitions.

> **bank** a. a place to keep money
>
> b. to use a bank
>
> c. the land next to a river

Which meaning of bank is used in each sentence?
Write the letter on the line.

1. The water ran onto the bank when it rained. ______

2. The bank was closed on Sunday. ______

3. My parents bank at Evermore Savings. ______

Write a sentence for each meaning of the word bank .

4. ____

____

5. ____

____

6. ____

____

Correct the sentences.

1. anna and tami are friends

____

2. them like to ride bikes

____

Write the missing words.

3. Anna wants _______________ to ride to _______________ house.

we   us   she   her

Circle two words that are (common nouns) .

4. Tami gave Anna a basket for her bike.

Correct the sentences.

1. did them go on the class trip to the farm

____

2. Me and Cam saw a friendly cow.

____

Write one more thing that (goes in the group) .

3. apples   oranges   peaches   _______________

Circle the (proper noun) .

4. his farm   Sunny Hill Farm   a big farm

Correct the sentences.

1. look careful before you cross the street

____

2. watch out for that there car

____

Write the missing word.

3. Use the crosswalk to _________________ to the other side.

get   git   gete

Circle the word that is the past tense of walk .

4. Ty walked across the street with Jen.

Correct the sentences.

1. Pigs is very smrt animals?

____

2. them roll in the mud to cool off

____

Circle two words that have the same meaning .

3. small   fast   little   long

Use but to write one sentence.

4. Pigs don't see well. Pigs hear well.

____

Read the adjectives.

> playful   striped   sharp

Write the adjective that goes in each sentence.

1. May I wear my _________________ shirt today?

2. The _________________ kitten ran to the toy mouse.

3. Be careful with the _________________ pencil.

Write a sentence using each adjective.

4. ____

____

5. ____

____

6. ____

____

Correct the sentences.

1. Lucas has math, spell, and reading home work.

____

2. Will you help he learn his spelling words

____

Write the missing word.

3. Lucas ________________ does his homework after school.
   silly   carefully   tired

Circle the word that means a group of people who do a sport together .

4. Then he will meet with his swim team.

Correct the sentences.

1. Last year, we growed pumpkins in our garden

____

2. We grew yellow white green and red ones.

____

Circle the word that means do not .

3. couldn't   don't   doesn't

Write the missing word.

4. We ________________ going to grow pumpkins again.
   is   are   our

Correct the sentences.

1. them girls like to ride horses

____

2. They go horseback rideing every saturday

____

Write the missing word.

3. Once they saw a _________________ of horses.

      herd   flock   pile

Circle the word that means cannot .

4. The girls are unhappy that they can't go next week.

Correct the sentences.

1. me and liam are best friends

____

2. him and me like cats and dogs alot.

____

Circle the word that is the opposite of soft .

3. fluffy   smooth   hard

Use and to write one sentence.

4. Liam has a big bulldog. Liam has an orange cat.

____

Read the words and their definitions.

art *noun*
a painting, a drawing, or something else made with your hands

artist *noun*
a person who makes art

artistic *adjective*
able to make art

Write the word that goes in each sentence.

1. My teacher is very _________________.

2. My mom is taking classes to be an _________________.

3. There is a beautiful piece of _________________ on the wall.

Use each word to write a sentence.

4. ____

____

5. ____

____

6. ____

____

Correct the sentences.

1. Where is they going on friday

____

2. they are going to the store to by striped socks

____

Write the missing date.

3. The sock store opened on _____________________.

      may 6 2014   May, 6 2014   May 6, 2014

Write the missing word.

4. sock : foot :: mitten : __________________

Correct the sentences.

1. my dad like to fix things

____

2. did he fixed the broken car

____

Use but to write one sentence.

3. He didn't fix the car yet. He fixed my bike.

____

Circle the word that means finish .

4. After I complete my homework, I will ride my bike.

Correct the sentences.

1. my sister liks the book <u>Little Red Riding Hood</u>?

____

2. this morning, she didnt know where it was

____

Write the missing word.

3. We looked _________________ for it.

    nowhere   everyone   everywhere

Use pile to finish the sentence.

4. We found the book under _______________________.

Correct the sentences.

1. can you name a animal that don't have no tail

____

2. an ape is an animal that doesn't have no tail

____

Write the missing word.

3. Read a book to _________________ more about animals.

    teach   learn   teacher

Circle the word that is spelled correctly.

4. cloce   close   cloose

Read the words and their definitions.

cent *noun*
a penny

sent *verb*
past tense of **send**

scent *noun*
a smell

Write the word that goes in each sentence.

1. The rose has a beautiful _________________.

2. A ball costs one _______________ less than a book.

3. I _________________ a card to my grandma.

Use each word to write a sentence.

4. ____

____

5. ____

____

6. ____

____

Correct the sentences.

1. Is logan the tall boy in the whole class

2. logans dad is tallest than we are

Use **because** **to write one sentence.**

3. Logan gave me his old shirt. His old shirt was too small for him.

Circle the word that means **known about by many people** **.**

4. Logan wants to be a famous singer some day.

Correct the sentences.

1. We saw a bear when we goed camp.

2. the bear ate for big fish

Read the sentences. Rewrite to make one sentence.

3. Bears can smell, see, and hear. Bears can do those things well.

Circle the word that means **a large number of** **.**

4. Many bears sleep all winter long.

Correct the sentences.

1. will you came to my house next thursday

____

2. I live next to the pond on beach road.

____

Circle the word that means more than one goose .

3. We can feed the geese and the ducks.

Write the missing word.

4. At ___________________, we can watch a movie.

2 ocl'ock   2 o'clock   2 oclock

Correct the sentences.

1. a bird maked a nest in hour front yard

____

2. did you see the bird ate a worm

____

Write the missing word.

3. Three birds were in the tree ______________ one flew away.

or   so   but

Circle two words that do not belong .

4. robin   airplane   blue jay   crow   kite

Read the words and their definitions.

> **bold** *adjective*
> not afraid; brave
>
> **boldly** *adverb*
> without fear
>
> **boldest** *adjective*
> the most bold

Write the word that goes in each sentence.

1. My sister ________________ swam across the pool.

2. The ________________ puppy in the litter ran to me.

3. A ________________ girl sang a song for her class.

Use each word to write a sentence.

4. ____

____

5. ____

____

6. ____

____

Correct the sentences.

1. They didnt get to go to lake george last summer

____

2. Them went to see Ant Patti at lake tahoe.

____

Write the missing word.

3. They _________________ there in an airplane.

    flied   flew   flyed

Circle the contraction that means I will .

4. i'll   Ill   I'll

Correct the sentences.

1. when is your sisters birthday

____

2. She was born on october 1 2013.

____

Write the missing word.

3. Your sister and _________________ have the same birthday.

        I   me   my

Write one more word that has th .

4. thin   birthday   _________________

Correct the sentences.

1. emma likes to ride her bike play ball and run

———————————————————————————————

2. Every day, her rides she's bike to school

———————————————————————————————

Circle two adjectives .

3. Emma is getting a new, bigger bike tomorrow.

Circle the plural words .

4. races   she's   berries

Correct the sentences.

1. Is we gonna have pizza for dinner.

———————————————————————————————

2. Ill help you mak it on friday at 4:30 p.m.

———————————————————————————————

Write the missing word.

3. _________________ going to taste so good!

    Its   It's   I'ts

Circle the word that is the opposite of cold .

4. wet   hat   dark   hot

Read the word and its definitions.

> **raise** a. to lift something up
>
>   b. to take care of children or animals until they are grown
>
>   c. to get money to help a group

Which meaning of raise is used in each sentence?
Write the letter on the line.

1. We are going to raise the kitten we found. ______

2. Raise your hand for a turn to speak. ______

3. Our class wants to raise money for guide dogs. ______

Write a sentence for each meaning of the word raise .

4. ____

____

5. ____

____

6. ____

____

Correct the sentences.

1. Last week, a horse jump over the tall wall

____

2. A ant cant jump over a tall wall, but it can clime.

____

Write the missing word.

3. A _________________ of birds flew over the tall wall.

    flock   herd   pack

Use the word **could** **to write a question.**

4. ____

Correct the sentences.

1. mrs. glenn piked up the crying baby.

____

2. her sang a song too make the baby laugh

____

Circle the word that means the same as **sad** .

3. happy   happily   unhappy

Circle two words that are **nouns** .

4. baby   sad   song   unhappy

Correct the sentences.

1. in the fall, it mite start to rain or snow.

____

2. Sum animals get redy for a long winter sleep.

____

Circle the words that go together .

3. snow   hill   rain   wind

Write the missing word.

4. _______________________ are animals that don't sleep all winter.

    Deers   Deer's   Deer

Correct the sentences.

1. What did beths puppy do

____

2. it chewed up dads hat.

____

Write a question about Beth's puppy.

3. ____

Write the missing word.

4. Let's buy the puppy some toys to keep it ________________.

                             busy   soft   small

Read the adverbs.

> happily   loudly   tightly

Write the adverb that goes in each sentence.

1. He _________________ closed his lunchbox.

2. All the students worked _________________ in groups.

3. The dog barked _________________ at the stranger.

Write a sentence using each adverb.

4. ____

____

5. ____

____

6. ____

____

Correct the sentences.

1. Should we aks if we can get a new pet

____

2. If we git a pet, w'ell take care of it

____

Circle the word that comes after cat in ABC order.

3. fish   dog   bird

Write the two words that are in goldfish .

4. _______________   _______________

Correct the sentences.

1. how many egg does your red hen lay

____

2. Last week my hen layed for eggs

____

Write the missing word.

3. _______________ you happy to have fresh eggs?

Ain't   Aren't   Isn't

Write the missing word.

4. wing : hen :: fin : _______________

Correct the sentences.

1. uncle ted catched six fish today.

____

2. lets go cook them fish.

____

Write the missing word.

3. Does ________________ want to help us?

anywhere   anyone   everywhere

Circle the word that can mean one or more than one of something.

4. campfire   fish   lake

Correct the sentences.

1. My friend at texas sended me a big box.

____

2. Whut was in side that big box

____

Use a noun to finish the sentence.

3. Inside that box was a funny ________________.

Circle the word that means something you know about .

4. Wow, I didn't expect that!

Read the word and its definitions.

> **right**   a. correct
>
>   b. the opposite of left
>
>   c. something the law says you can do

Which meaning of right is used in each sentence?
Write the letter on the line.

1. My mom and dad have the right to vote.   _______

2. You had the right answer to the math problem.   _______

3. Turn right at the next street.   _______

Write a sentence for each meaning of the word right .

4. ____

    ____

5. ____

    ____

6. ____

    ____

Correct the sentences.

1. dr. ross told Ava that its good to exercise every day.

____

2. She ride her bike every where she can

____

Write the missing word.

3. _______________________ bike is the purple one.

Avas   Ava   Ava's

Circle the abbreviation for Mister .

4. Mrs.   Mr.   Dr.

Correct the sentences.

1. does you like sports

____

2. I like to play baseball with Gabe Mia and Alex?

____

Use the words small and white to rewrite the sentence.

3. We hit the baseball.

____

Circle the words that go together .

4. soccer   baseball   dance   football

Correct the sentences.

1. on monday, i saw a frog at the park on elm street

____

2. It was green and haved spots on it's back

____

Use because to write one sentence.

3. I like frogs. I like to see them hop.

____

Write one more word that has the sound of g in frog .

4. grass   tag   _______________________

Correct the sentences.

1. pick Juans gacket up off the floor.

____

2. carefully dust moms vase.

____

Use stairs and down to make a compound word.

3. ____

Write the opposite .

4. clean   _______________________

Read the words and their definitions.

friend *noun*
a person that you know and like

friendly *adjective*
showing kind feelings

friendship *noun*
the close feeling between friends

Write the word that goes in each sentence.

1. My ________________ sits next to me in class.

2. Lily and I have a great ________________.

3. The ________________ boy helped me after I fell.

Use each word to write a sentence.

4. ____

____

5. ____

____

6. ____

____

Correct the sentences.

1. I seen a yellow kitten goed under the house

____

2. I tryed to catch it, but it was to fast

____

Write the missing word.

3. The kitten _________________ out of my hands.

    jumped   jump   jumping

Circle the word that means needing food .

4. The kitten will come out when it is hungry.

Correct the sentences.

1. Did Joel David and Jack go to Ryan's house

____

2. They want to sea Ryans new game

____

Circle the question that is informal .

3. What's up?   How are you?

Circle the name that comes before David in ABC order.

4. Jack   Ryan   Carlos

Correct the sentences.

1. On saturday we are flying to florida

____

2. we will take a taxi to the Airport

____

Write the missing word.

3. We ______________________ in an airplane last year.

rided   rode   roded

Write the missing word.

4. taxi : ground :: airplane : ______________________

Correct the sentences.

1. Honeybees help many plant grows.

____

2. Sum bees cary pollen from one flower to another

____

Circle the word that names a group of bees .

3. pack   swarm   flock

Circle the word that means to keep safe .

4. Worker bees find food and protect the hive.

Read the verbs and their definitions.
Each verb tells about a stronger action than the one before it.

toss	to throw in an easy way
throw	to send through the air from your hand
hurl	to throw very hard and carelessly

Write the verb that goes in each sentence.

1. She can gently _________________ the ball to the puppy.

2. Don't _________________ your shoe out the window!

3. He will _________________ the ball to first base.

Use each verb to write a sentence.

4. ____

____

5. ____

____

6. ____

____

Correct the sentences.

1. Did you ever seen a oak tree?

____

2. Some oaks trees can grow to bee 80 foot tall.

____

Write the missing word.

3. Oak trees lose their _____________________ in the fall.

　　　　　　leafs　　　leaves　　　leafes

Circle the word that means　cover from the sun　.

4. On a hot day, you can rest in the shade of an oak tree.

Correct the sentences.

1. Many peopl like to eat yam in the Fall.

____

2. Sum yams grow on africa.

____

Use　commas　and the word　and　to write one sentence.

3. My mom likes yams. My dad likes yams. I like yams.

____

Use　He　or　She　to finish the sentence.

4. Mom cooked yams. _______________ roasted them in the oven.

Correct the sentences.

1. Jon ran in a race on saturday June 21 2014.

____

2. He ran every monday wednesday and friday to get ready for it.

____

Circle the word that does not belong .

3. run   eat   swim   walk

Circle the sentence that is formal .

4. Wanna play with me?   Do you want to play with me?

Correct the sentences.

1. don't touches that hot stove

____

2. can you help mom mix the pancake batter

____

Read the sentences. Use so to make one sentence.

3. I will wash my hands. I can help if I wash my hands.

____

Circle the plural words .

4. hands   hand's   feet   foots

Read the adverbs.

> always   carefully   never

Write an adverb in each sentence.

1. It _________________ snows in our city.

2. We _________________ go to Grandma's house for spring break.

3. Dad _________________ fixed Mom's broken vase.

Write a sentence using each adverb.

4. ____

____

5. ____

____

6. ____

____

Correct the sentences.

1. My grandma went to new york last Winter.

____

2. she took a taxi to central park.

____

Write the missing word.

3. She saw _________________ riding sleds in the snow.

    childs   children   childrens

Read the sentences. Use and to write one sentence.

4. My grandma went out to dinner. My grandma saw a play.

____

Correct the sentences.

1. mouses are tiny animals weth long tales.

____

2. They can be white brown or gray

____

Circle the word that means twelve .

3. A mother mouse can have a dozen babies every three weeks.

Circle the word that comes before mouse in ABC order.

4. rat   lion   tiger   mule

Correct the sentences.

1. The two ladys went shopping in portland oregon.

____

2. Then thay went to mt. hood for a hike.

____

Circle the meaning of the underlined word.

3. They want to <u>revisit</u> Oregon again next year.

    fly there   visit again   not visit

Circle the sentence that is informal .

4. Goodbye, Sara.   Catch ya later.

Correct the sentences.

1. Kim isnt hear at school today because shes ill.

____

2. Ill ask the teacher if we can make card for her

____

Write the missing word.

3. We hope ______________________ feel better soon.

    she'll   she'ill   her'll

Circle the word that is spelled correctly.

4. eny   iny   any

Read the word and its definitions.

> **seal**
> a. a sea animal that has four flippers
> b. to close something up
> c. a picture stamped onto important papers

Which meaning of seal is used in each sentence?
Write the letter on the line.

1. Seal the letter before you mail it. ______

2. The king's seal is on his letter to the queen. ______

3. The seal swam around the boat. ______

Write a sentence using each meaning of the word seal .

4. ____

____

5. ____

____

6. ____

____

Correct the sentences.

1. Does Ms. Clark work in denver colorado

____

2. Her son José, is on the same team as me.

____

Write the missing date.

3. We went to a baseball game on _________________________.

       Friday July, 11 2013   Friday, July 11, 2013

Circle the words that go together .

4. team   group   crowd   herd

Correct the sentences.

1. We are think uv getting a pet turtle

____

2. Can you tell us hau two take care of a turtle?

____

Write the missing word.

3. Is a turtle _________________ than a snail?

    slow   slower   slowest

Circle the sentence that is formal .

4. Thanks for helping out.   Thank you for helping us.

Correct the sentences.

1. i am reading my knew book abowt snakes.

____

2. i didn't know that snakes doesn't have eyelids.

____

Read the sentences. Use so to write one sentence.

3. Snakes can't bite their food. They have to swallow it whole.

____

Circle the word that means don't agree .

4. My sister thinks snakes are awful, but I disagree.

Correct the sentences.

1. Do your family have a speshul dinner for thanksgiving?

____

2. grandma is coming to be with us for kwanzaa

____

Read the sentences. Use if to write one sentence.

3. I can be in the Halloween parade. I have to make a mask first.

____

Circle the words that need a capital letter .

4. hanukkah   birthday   christmas   new year's day

Read the nouns.

Singular	Plural
button	buttons
peach	peaches
man	men

Write the noun that goes in each sentence.

1. A ________________ fell off my shirt.

2. Those ________________ are my dad's friends.

3. I picked a ________________ from the tree.

Write a sentence using each plural noun.

4. ____

____

5. ____

____

6. ____

____

Correct the sentences.

1. Do you write a letter to mr. ruiz yet?

____

2. please thank him for finding our dog, toby

____

Write the missing word.

3. Why _________________ the backyard gate closed?

weren't   was'nt   wasn't

Circle the word that means join again .

4. enjoy   joiner   rejoin

Correct the sentences.

1. Kris just learnt how to make cookys.

____

2. Kriss mom helpt her make some last saturday.

____

Read the sentences. Use so **to write one sentence.**

3. Kris is going to a party. She made extra cookies to take.

____

Circle the adjectives .

4. The happy children liked the warm, tasty cookies.

Correct the sentences.

1. we need to bee there buy 6 oclock.

____

2. Hurry, we cant be late

____

Write the missing word.

3. _____________________ put on your shoes and socks!

Quick   Quicker   Quickly

Circle the word that is spelled correctly .

4. wif   with   wiht

Correct the sentences.

1. the farmer went in to the barn dis morning

____

2. there was a lot of mouses in the barn.

____

Write one more word that goes in the group .

3. pink   gray   tan   _______________

Circle the word that comes after mouse in ABC order.

4. man   mug   mitt

Read the words and their definitions.

> **hurry** *verb*
> to do things as fast as you can
>
> **hurried** *adjective*
> done in a hurry; rushed
>
> **unhurried** *adjective*
> done slowly

Write the word that goes in each sentence.

1. The day was _________________, with too many things to do.

2. We like to be _________________ when we walk through the zoo.

3. I will _________________ so we won't be late!

Use each word to write a sentence.

4. ____

____

5. ____

____

6. ____

____

Correct the sentences.

1. Maria wanted to grow lettuce beets an carrots.

____

2. Her garden wus in the backyard bye the fence.

____

Circle the meaning of the underlined word.

3. Maria made small holes in the <u>soil</u> before she planted the seeds.

rocks　　　dirt　　　weeds

Circle the sentence that is informal .

4. Please calm down.　　　Chill out.

Correct the sentences.

1. Why isnt Jesses bike at his house

____

2. He's bike need new tires, so its at the shop.

____

Write the missing word.

3. He ___________________ know what to do without it.

doesn't　　　can't　　　don't

Circle the word that means almost the same as thinking .

4. Jesse is dreaming of getting a new bike someday.

Correct the sentences.

1. i and amy like stories about elfs.

____

2. Sometimes a elf can get into a litle trouble

____

Write the missing word.

3. Did you see the elf _________________ in the garden?

       dances   dancing   dancer

Write the missing word.

4. in : out :: up : _________________

Correct the sentences.

1. Dr. lopez lives in a white house at 245 robin road.

____

2. he lives in the Country, but he works in the sity.

____

Use the word beautiful to rewrite the sentence.

3. Dr. Lopez likes to work in his garden.

____

Circle three words that have the sound of c in city .

4. cent   coat   circle   cell

Read the adjectives and their definitions.
Each adjective describes a noun in a stronger way than the one before it.

thin	not very thick
slender	thin and graceful
scrawny	too thin

Write the adjective that goes in each sentence.

1. I cut a small, _________________ slice of cake.

2. We took the _________________ puppy home to feed him.

3. The flower grew on a tall, _________________ stem.

Use each adjective to write a sentence.

4. ____

____

5. ____

____

6. ____

____

Correct the sentences.

1. did you see the butterfly sat on that flower

____

2. i red that many butterflys taste with their feet.

____

Write the missing word.

3. A _______________________ wings often have bright colors.

butterflies   butterfly's   butterflys

Circle the word that means almost the same as travel .

4. Some butterflies migrate to a place very far away.

Correct the sentences.

1. The teacher read <u>charlotte's web</u> to the class in january

____

2. I read <u>green eggs and ham</u> to my little brother last night.

____

Use too or two to finish the sentence.

3. He is _______________ years old, and he loves books.

Read the sentences. Use or to write one sentence.

4. Some books can make me laugh. Some books can make me cry.

Correct the sentences.

1. were going to canada in may.

____

2. we will go to a city near the pacific ocean.

____

Write the word that is the opposite of going .

3. ___________________

Circle the words that need a capital letter .

4. april   sunday   fish   victoria

Correct the sentences.

1. Grasshoppers are usually gray brown or green

____

2. most grasshopper have large eye.

____

Write the missing word.

3. Have you seen a grasshopper ___________ a cricket?

or   if   so

Circle the words that go together .

4. bee   snake   ant   grasshopper

Read the word and its definitions.

> **step**　a. placing one foot ahead while walking
>
> b. a place to put your foot when going up or down stairs
>
> c. one thing you do in a series

Which meaning of step is used in each sentence?
Write the letter on the line.

1. The first step is to read the directions.　______

2. Be careful when you get to the top step.　______

3. Step over the puddle on the sidewalk.　______

Write a sentence for each meaning of the word step .

4. ____

____

5. ____

____

6. ____

____

Correct the sentences.

1. Our family will go to york maine next month.

   ____

2. Well play at the beach and eat fresh sea food

   ____

Write the missing word.

3. Dad will buy _____________________ a new camera to take.

   myself   himself   herself

Circle the word that means cannot .

4. My brother and I can't wait to go!

Correct the sentences.

1. Deon blue up a blew balloon.

   ____

2. He gave it to his little sister, sara.

   ____

Make this a complete sentence.

3. When she let go of the balloon ___________________________.

Use a or an to finish the sentence.

4. Next time, Deon wants to get _____________ orange balloon.

Correct the sentences.

1. Kyle lives in 623 Toro Road, medford oregon.

   ____

2. Tim lives round the corner on main street.

   ____

Write the missing word.

3. They both got new _________________ last week.

        puppes   puppys   puppies

Circle the adverb.

4. quick   quickly   quickest   quicker

Correct the sentences.

1. Tomorrow was my brothers first day of swimming.

   ____

2. He will swim from 3:00 to 4:00 at the avalon swim center

   ____

Use across or against to finish the sentence.

3. He will swim _________________ the pool.

Rewrite the sentence in a different order.

4. Swimming is the sport he likes best.

   He likes ____

Read the adjectives and adverbs.

Adjectives	Adverbs
busy	busily
noisy	noisily
sudden	suddenly

Write the adjective or adverb that goes with the underlined word.

1. ________________, a big spider <u>jumped</u> on me!

2. The dog <u>barked</u> ________________ at the cat.

3. My <u>mom</u> was too ________________ to bake cookies today.

Write a sentence using the adjective or adverb.

busily

4. ____

____

noisy

5. ____

____

sudden

6. ____

____

Correct the sentences.

1. Many people eats watermelon evry summer.

____

2. if you tap on a watermelon, i'tll sounds like a drum.

____

Write the missing word.

3. I would like a _________________ watermelon right now!

     juicy   hugely   noisy

Use (they) to rewrite the sentence without names.

4. Siri and Alena like to eat watermelon, too.

____

Correct the sentences.

1. Kai loosed two tooths last friday.

____

2. Thay falled out during lunch, after he ate a apple.

____

Use (because) to write one sentence.

3. Kai is happy. The Tooth Fairy is coming.

____

Circle the word that is (spelled correctly).

4. nearlie   nearly   neerly

Correct the sentences.

1. Why is dad going to dallas, texas?

____

2. Hes going to paint grandmas house.

____

Write the missing word.

3. He's also going to paint her ______________ house.

dogs   dog'es   dog's

Circle the word that means paint again .

4. painting   repaint   painter   paints

Correct the sentences.

1. can Marco count to ten in spanish

____

2. Can he read the story to kali and I

____

Circle the verbs .

3. Marco counted, read a book, and gave us a big grin.

Write the missing word.

4. Marco felt very proud of ______________.

himself   hisself   he

Read the words and their definitions.

> **help**   *verb*
> to do something that is needed
>
> **helpful**   *adjective*
> giving help
>
> **helpless**   *adjective*
> not able to take care of oneself

Write the word that goes in each sentence.

1. Please ________________ Grandpa pull weeds in the garden.

2. The puppy was ________________ without its mother.

3. It was ________________ when you washed the dishes.

Use each word to write a sentence.

4. ____

____

5. ____

____

6. ____

____

Correct the sentences.

1. Long ago, persons made baskets to karry there things.

____

2. baskets were made out of wood grasses or vines.

____

Circle the word that means people who make .

3. Basket makers used things they found outside.

Circle the word that is spelled correctly .

4. fastur   fastr   faster

Correct the sentences.

1. wild horses liv in groups called herds

____

2. Beeing in a herd helps wyld horse's stay safe.

____

Use and **to write one sentence.**

3. Wild horses eat grasses all day. Wild horses eat other plants all day.

____

Circle the words that show possession .

4. the horse's tail   three boys   Kim's horse

Correct the sentences.

1. Wat type of berry do you like best

____

2. Eye like blueberrys the best

____

Write the missing word.

3. You can grow berries _________________.

　　　　　yourself　　　myself　　　itself

Use **with** **or** **during** **to finish the sentence.**

4. You can buy fresh berries _____________ the summer.

Correct the sentences.

1. Please gimme a orange.

____

2. I beginned eating healthy snak ever day.

____

Circle the words that mean picked **by a person** **.**

3. Most oranges are picked by hand.

Circle the word that is **spelled correctly** **.**

4. pushe　　　puch　　　push

Read the words and their definitions.

> **road** *noun*
> a wide path for cars and people
>
> **rode** *verb*
> past tense of **ride**
>
> **rowed** *verb*
> past tense of **row**

Write the word that goes in each sentence.

1. We ________________ the boat using wooden oars.

2. My mom drove on the long ________________ to the city.

3. I ________________ my bike to my friend's house.

Use each word to write a sentence.

4. ____

   ____

5. ____

   ____

6. ____

   ____

Correct the sentences.

1. a robin made a nest in are peach tree

____

2. The Mother robin layed three eggs.

____

Write the missing word.

3. When will _______________ baby birds come out?

    them   those   they

Circle the opposites .

4. loud   huge   quiet

Correct the sentences.

1. My family likes to go fishing at pine lake every sumer.

____

2. evan said he doesn't never get to go fishing

____

Use but to write one sentence.

3. Evan can come with us. He must bring his own fishing pole.

____

Write the contraction .

4. will not   _______________

Correct the sentences.

1. polar bares live in the icy cold arctic

____

2. Them have blubber an thick fur that keeps them warm

____

Circle the word that means the bottom of feet .

3. Polar bears' feet have bumpy soles that grip the ice.

Rewrite the sentence using the word slowly .

4. Polar bears walk across the slippery ice.

____

Correct the sentences.

1. How many childs are in your class

____

2. Well ask everyone to come to the party on friday may 2

____

Circle the words that name insects .

3. be   bee   ant   aunt

Circle the meaning of we're .

4. were   we are   we will

Read the nouns.

Singular	Plural
pony	ponies
life	lives
person	people

Write the noun that goes in each sentence.

1. One spotted _________________ ate grass on the hill.

2. Our _________________ are busy on school days.

3. Three _________________ were waiting in line.

Write a sentence using each plural noun.

4. ____

____

5. ____

____

6. ____

____

Correct the sentences.

1. Ant Tina growed roses and daisys in her garden.

____

2. On friday she put sum flowers in a vase.

____

Write the missing word.

3. Aunt _________________ garden is beautiful!

   Tina   Tinas   Tina's

Circle the word that comes first in ABC order.

4. rose   daisy   sunflower

Correct the sentences.

1. Did you now that a octopus can change it's color?

____

2. most octopuses live in warm parts ov the oshun.

____

Use so to write one sentence.

3. Octopuses spray dark ink. Then they can get away from danger.

____

Use itself or themselves to finish the sentence.

4. Octopuses can hide _________________ in the rocks.

Correct the sentences.

1. When can him and i have a turn on the bars

____

2. Thank you four shareing with us

____

Write the missing word.

3. When you share, you are being a ________________ friend.

                          silly   selfish   kind

Circle the words that have the same meaning.

4. friend   stranger   pal

Correct the sentences.

1. Carla has went to big pine Camp last summer.

____

2. She done learned how to row a boat awn the lake

____

Circle the words that are adjectives.

3. cold   slowly   fast   blue

Rewrite the sentence using two adjectives.

4. Carla likes to swim in the lake.

____

Read the verbs and their definitions. Each verb tells about a stronger action.

whisper	to speak very softly with your breath and no voice
talk	to say words or speak
shout	to talk or cry out in a very loud voice

Write the verb that goes in each sentence.

1. Please _________________ so you don't wake the baby.

2. You can _________________ for your team at the ballgame.

3. _________________ to your partner about the math problem.

Use each verb to write a sentence.

4. ____

____

5. ____

____

6. ____

____

Correct the sentences.

1. Theres a flock of wild turkey's standing on the hill.

   ____

2. Last friday, they walk around our yard

   ____

Write the missing word.

3. A turkey's gobble can be _________________ far away.

   heard   heared   herd

Circle the words that mean eat .

4. Turkeys feed on nuts, seeds, berries, and insects.

Correct the sentences.

1. Why do some people likes to run for exercise

   ____

2. some people like runing because they can do it outdoors.

   ____

Use you or yourself to finish the sentence.

3. If you want to run, buy _________________ a pair of running shoes.

Circle the adverbs .

4. We will cheer loudly for you if you run quickly.

Correct the sentences.

1. what are some sign that spring is coming

____

2. There is flours growing and bird's singing.

____

Write the missing word.

3. Spring has ________________!

    sprang   springed   sprung

Use time and spring to make a compound word.

4. ________________________________

Correct the sentences.

1. Last august I readed <u>Frog and Toad Together</u>.

____

2. I cant wait to read another book by arnold lobel.

____

Use the adverb happily and the adjective funny to write a new sentence.

3. I read books!

____

Use reread or reader to finish the sentence.

4. My little brother can read now, so he is a ________________.

Read the word and its definitions.

> **top**   a. the highest part of something
>
>   b. a lid or cover
>
>   c. a shirt

Which meaning of top is used in each sentence?
Write the letter on the line.

1. Please put the top on the jar.   _______

2. We walked to the top of the hill.   _______

3. That top looks nice with those pants.   _______

Write a sentence for each meaning of the word top .

4. ____

    ____

5. ____

    ____

6. ____

    ____

Correct the sentences.

1. Is we gonna go to Cape Cod this fall

____

2. we can ride on a boat to go sea an island

____

Circle the word that means more than one leaf .

3. I hope we will be able to see the colorful fall leaves.

Write the missing word.

4. smile : happy :: frown : _____________________

Correct the sentences.

1. Dani don't want to wach that movie

____

2. Julies Mom said we can ride our bikes instead.

____

Circle the adverb that tells how .

3. We will gladly ride on the bike path.

Circle the word that is spelled correctly .

4. stoud   stood   stude

Correct the sentences.

1. Last sunday we see wild rabits.

____

2. Sumtimes we see them wen we go four walks.

____

Circle the adverb that tells when .

3. I saw a rabbit run into a hole yesterday.

Rewrite the sentence in a different order.

4. When the rabbit saw us coming, it ran away.

The rabbit ____

Correct the sentences.

1. Our Dad read ramona the pest with us.

____

2. Sometime my little sister is like ramona

____

Circle the words that tell the action .

3. My little sister goes to kindergarten.

Circle the adverb that tells how they try .

4. Ramona and my sister really try to do their best, but it isn't easy.

Read the adjectives and adverbs.

Adjectives	Adverbs
bright	brightly
firm	firmly
slow	slowly

Write the adjective or adverb that goes with each underlined word.

1. A snail <u>went</u> _________________ across the sidewalk.

2. The sun <u>shone</u> _________________ on the garden.

3. We need a _________________ <u>ball</u> to play soccer.

Write a sentence using each adjective or adverb.

bright

4. ____

____

firmly

5. ____

____

slow

6. ____

____

Correct the sentences.

1. My parents was marryed on june 20 2008

____

2. Mom said it were a beautiful suny hot summer day

____

Write the missing word.

3. The _______________ family was there.

   hole   whole   wole

Use tasty and lively to rewrite the sentence.

4. Then they had a party with music and food.

____

Correct the sentences.

1. What was they doing in dr winn's backyard?

____

2. They were helping him plant punkin seads?

____

Use so to write one sentence.

3. We are planting the seeds now. There will be pumpkins in the fall.

____

Circle the word that means land next to a house .

4. Dr. Winn has many plants growing in his yard.

Correct the sentences.

1. i sees dark clouds floating slowly in the skie.

   ____

2. Does it mean that its going to rain today.

   ____

Circle the word that tells **who** .

3. Riley can wear his new raincoat.

Write the two words that are in **raindrop** .

4. _______________   _______________

Correct the sentences.

1. Dont play with that sharp knife

   ____

2. Aks your mom to putt it safely away.

   ____

Circle the word that **comes last** **in ABC order.**

3. spoon   fork   knife   napkin

Write the missing word.

4. How many forks, spoons, and _______________ do we need?

                   knife   knifes   knives

Read the words and their definitions.

> **kind** *adjective*
> helpful; friendly
>
> **unkind** *adjective*
> not helpful or friendly
>
> **kindness** *noun*
> a kind act

Write the word that goes in each sentence.

1. The boy showed _________________ when he helped a lost kitten.

2. Kayla is _________________ to others when she offers her seat.

3. It would be _________________ to leave a mess on the floor.

Use each word to write a sentence.

4. ____

____

5. ____

____

6. ____

____

Correct the sentences.

1. We taked owr dog for a walk before we feeded him.

____

2. When i grow up, im going to bee a vet.

____

Write the contraction .

3. did not _______________________

Circle the sentence that is informal .

4. See ya later.   Goodbye, Kim.

Correct the sentences.

1. Masons Dad builded a tall fence.

____

2. Than he paint it brown.

____

Circle the word that means had a quick look .

3. He glanced at the dog that was staring through the fence.

Use -er to write a word that means a person who paints .

4. paint___________

Correct the sentences.

1. When did Mr. ruiz learned to fly a airplane?

____

2. He start going to flight school on may 6 2014.

____

Write the missing word.

3. Mr. Ruiz hopes that he can fly _________________ to Alaska.

         hisself   him   himself

Circle the word that means **to keep a record of** .

4. He has to log all his practice flying hours.

Correct the sentences.

1. her and me went to see some kittens.

____

2. Whats the white kittens name

____

Use **or** **to write one sentence.**

3. Do you want a puppy? Do you want a kitten?

____

Circle the word that tells **who is sleeping** .

4. The kitten is sleeping on my sister's lap.

Read the nouns.

Singular	Plural
child	children
fish	fish
mouse	mice

Write the noun that goes in each sentence.

1. Five orange _________________ swam in the pond.

2. One _________________ was late to the party.

3. A tiny _________________ ran across the floor.

Write a sentence using each plural noun.

4. ____

____

5. ____

____

6. ____

____

Correct the sentences.

1. I am haveing salad, chicken, and a apple four lunch.

____

2. My dad likes to ate a biggest lunch then I do.

____

Write the missing word.

3. Jake _________________ a cheese, lettuce, and tomato sandwich.

      gots   has   is

Write like or love in each sentence.

4. I _________________ my dad.   I _________________ my lunch.

Correct the sentences.

1. My ant works in the bank over they're

____

2. She don't go to work on Saturday's or Sunday's.

____

Circle the words that tell what the aunt does .

3. My aunt counts money at work.

Write the opposite .

4. low   _________________

Correct the sentences.

1. Jon didn't do nothing bad.

   ____

2. He triped over a crack in the side walk.

   ____

Write the missing word.

3. His lunchbox _________________ in the puddle.
   falled   felt   fell

Use but to write one sentence.

4. Today was not easy. Tomorrow will be better.

   ____

Correct the sentences.

1. Sea otter have thik fur that keep them warm.

   ____

2. Them floats together in groups caled rafts.

   ____

Circle the verbs .

3. Sea otters clean and groom their fur a lot.

Write the pronoun for the underlined word.

4. <u>Mike</u> saw a sea otter at the harbor. _____________

Read the verbs and their definitions.

clean	to make something neat and tidy
wipe	to get dirt off by rubbing
wash	to get dirt off with soap and water

Write the verb that goes in each sentence.

1. Get the soap, and we will _________________ the dog in a big tub.

2. I used a rag to _________________ the table.

3. If you _________________ your room, you can find your shoes.

Use each verb to write a sentence.

4. ____

   ____

5. ____

   ____

6. ____

   ____

Correct the sentences.

1. we saw a brown hawk siting on top of a pole.

____

2. Hawks make larje nests out off stick.

____

Write the missing word.

3. Hawks travel _______________ groups called casts or kettles.

       in   on   from

Circle the collective nouns .

4. A crowd of people watched the kettle of hawks flying south.

Correct the sentences.

1. Ever summer, mom gets out our i scream maker.

____

2. She makes ice cream with berries peaches or mangoes

____

Write the missing words.

3. Yesterday _____________ bought _____________ a new cookbook.

      she   her   her   herself

Circle the sentence that is formal .

4. It's so cool!   Making ice cream is really fun!

Correct the sentences.

1. Goats is very good jumper and climber.

   ____

2. Some goat clime trees or tal mountains.

   ____

Circle the meaning of the underlined word .

3. The <u>nimble</u> goat hopped up the steep cliff.

   moving quickly and lightly   moving slowly and heavily

Write a question about goats.

4. ____

Correct the sentences.

1. Las night my mom lighted ate candles.

   ____

2. Did you notice that a candles flam always points up

   ____

Write the missing word.

3. Mom says we can make _________________ some candles.

   ourselves   yourselves   themselves

Circle the word that means almost the same as make .

4. find   buy   build   take

Read the word and its definitions.

> **set** a. to put something in a place
>
>   b. ready
>
>   c. a group of things that go
>   together

Which meaning of set is used in each sentence?
Write the letter on the line.

1. Let's use our new set of dishes for dinner.   ______

2. Please set the book on the shelf.   ______

3. We are all set to go to the beach.   ______

Write a sentence for each meaning of the word set .

4. ____

____

5. ____

____

6. ____

____

Correct the sentences.

1. Hour rooster crow at 5:30 thise morning.

____

2. Evry day it crow just be fore sunrise.

____

Write the missing word.

3. How much do your ___________________ eat in one day?

    chicken's   chickens   chicken

Circle the collective nouns .

4. The flock of chickens ate the pile of feed.

Correct the sentences.

1. Long ago, people brought orange seads to america

____

2. I red that the first oranges were growed in florida.

____

Circle the meaning of the underlined word .

3. I like to learn the <u>history</u> of how things began.

    what happened in the past   a fairy tale

Circle the word that comes after orange in ABC order.

4. banana   peach   kiwi

Correct the sentences.

1. in tha Spring, it can be warm or cold outside.

____

2. Sometime its still cold enough to snow

____

Write the missing word.

3. Some spring days are very _______________________.

windy   windier   windiest

Circle the word that tells who likes to fly kites .

4. On a nice spring day, we like to fly kites.

Correct the sentences.

1. Uncle Mike lives in bend, oregon.

____

2. I wrote a leter asking him to vizit us on june 1.

____

Rewrite the sentence in a different order.

3. He can drive or fly to our house.

He can _______________________________________

Circle the words that need capital letters .

4. uncle   auntie marti   fun cousin   grandpa joe

Read the adjectives and adverbs.

Adjectives	Adverbs
lonely	soon
blue	always
furry	very

Write the adjective or adverb that goes with each underlined word.

1. We _________________ <u>go</u> to the park on Sundays.

2. Amy wants to wear her _________________ <u>dress</u> to the party.

3. We made friends with the _________________ <u>boy</u>.

Write a sentence with each word you did not use.

furry

4. ____

____

soon

5. ____

____

very

6. ____

____

Correct the sentences.

1. Yesterday, we see uh fox with a bushy tail.

____

2. it had read fur and white on the tip of it's tail.

____

Write the missing word.

3. Some foxes can run _________________ 30 miles in an hour.

       near   nearest   nearly

Circle the word that means tricky .

4. In fairy tales, foxes are known to be sly.

Correct the sentences.

1. Adam travis and ana went out to eat in the City.

____

2. They eated at a old place on Main street.

____

Circle the adjective .

3. Then they quickly rode bikes to a lovely park.

Rewrite the sentence in a different order.

4. Tomorrow they will fly home.

    They will _______________________________________

Correct the sentences.

1. tow big spider runned across the sidewalk.

____

2. they scard my little sister

____

Write the missing word.

3. A spider __________________ want to be near us, either.

     don't   isn't   doesn't

Circle the word that comes after spider in ABC order.

4. sand   sudden   silly

Correct the sentences.

1. my silly cat like too nap everywhere.

____

2. Once she sleeped with her head on moms shoe.

____

Circle the meaning of the underlined word .

3. Don't <u>trip</u> over my cat!

     travel for fun   hit your foot and fall

Circle the date that is written correctly.

4. july 20 1969   September 17, 1787   December 17 1903

Read the words and their definitions.

care *verb*
to feel that something is important

careful *adjective*
taking care so that there are no mistakes

caring *adjective*
showing kindness for others

Write the word that goes in each sentence.

1. When you help your sister, it shows that you _________________.

2. The _________________ girl shared her cookies.

3. Be _________________ when you wash the glass.

Use each word to write a sentence.

4. ____

____

5. ____

____

6. ____

____

Correct the sentences.

1. How many shelfs do we need to hold all are books

____

2. i think we need abowt five er six shelves.

____

Write the missing word.

3. That shelf is not big enough _______________ the math books.

                 for   four   if

Use **because** **to write one sentence.**

4. Don't put books on the high shelf. I can't reach them.

____

Correct the sentences.

1. Is the bike shop on maple street or west road?

____

2. My brothers bike tire need to be fixd.

____

Use the contraction for **will not** **to rewrite the sentence.**

3. I hope the tire will not cost too much money.

____

Circle the word that is the **opposite of first** **.**

4. second   last   after   best

Correct the sentences.

1. uncle tom likes to watch birds

____

2. He nose about the birds that live around he's house

____

Write the missing word.

3. He saw three hawks ______________ Tuesday.

at   in   on

Circle the collective nouns .

4. He saw a flock of robins on the grass after a shower of rain.

Correct the sentences.

1. What did you do wen you went to mexico

____

2. we went to the beech all most every day.

____

Circle the meaning of the underlined word .

3. We saw <u>divers</u> spring from a cliff into the sea.

people who dive   people who see a cliff

Write the two words that are in the word seashell .

4. ______________ ______________

Read the nouns.

Singular	Plural
woman	women
tooth	teeth
sheep	sheep

Write the noun that goes in each sentence.

1. I brushed my _________________ after dinner.

2. The _________________ with the brown hair is my mom.

3. Six _________________ were eating grass on the hill.

Write a sentence using each plural noun.

4. ____

____

5. ____

____

6. ____

____

Correct the sentences.

1. Our family moved frum utah to florida

____

2. We has lived in florida for two year.

____

Write the missing word.

3. Mom _________________, "It's nice to have old and new friends."
   sayed   saying   said

Circle the word that means met in a friendly way .

4. The people in Florida welcomed us to our new home.

Correct the sentences.

1. grandpa joe was a taxi driver.

____

2. for 30 years, he drive people around boston.

____

Rewrite the sentence in a different order.

3. Five years ago, a famous actor rode in his taxi.

   A famous actor _______________________________

Write the contraction .

4. I am _______________

Correct the sentences.

1. My pencil isnt working well

____

2. May I please sharpen it

____

Circle the complete sentence.

3. Two yellow pencils in my desk.   I lost my extra pencil.

Circle the meaning of the underlined word.

4. <u>Follow</u> me over to the new pencil sharpener.

go after   go ahead of   go first

Correct the sentences.

1. Erics school opened on august 11 2014.

____

2. it has a garden space weth a greenhouse.

____

Use tomorrow and large to rewrite the sentence.

3. Eric wants to work in the garden.

____

Circle the sentence that is formal .

4. We will begin working now.   Let's get to work!

Read the adjectives and their definitions.

happy	feeling sunny and pleased
joyful	very happy, full of joy
jolly	full of fun

Write the adjective that goes in each sentence.

1. The funny, _________________ clown made everyone laugh.

2. The children sang a _________________ song.

3. I feel _________________ when I read a good book.

Use each adjective to write a sentence.

4. ____

____

5. ____

____

6. ____

____

Correct the sentences.

1. Carlos and amy wanted to take the dog for uh walk

____

2. It beginned to rain when themselves went out side.

____

Write the missing words.

3. _________________ ran home as fast as they could.

Him and her   He and she

Circle the word that means it is **.**

4. It's too bad the dog got its fur wet.

Correct the sentences.

1. We lik to eat outdoor on uh warm day

____

2. Did some flys land on the table

____

Circle the adjectives **.**

3. Mom will put the bright red tablecloth on the big table.

Write the opposite **.**

4. outside   _________________

Correct the sentences.

1. how many crayons do you got

____

2. I gots a box of eighteen crayons

____

Write the missing word.

3. _______________ color do you like best?

Why   Where   Which

Circle the **nouns** .

4. My big brother has a box of thirty-six crayons.

Correct the sentences.

1. my dad and me pull weeds in the yard on saturday

____

2. than we planted purple and pink flours.

____

Use **lightly** **and** **colorful** **to rewrite the sentence.**

3. We sprayed water on the flowers.

____

Circle the words that **go together** .

4. garden   seeds   game   flowers

Read the word and its definitions.

> **fall** a. to drop down suddenly
>
>   b. to happen
>
>   c. the time of the year between summer and winter

Which meaning of fall is used in each sentence?
Write the letter on the line.

1. Some trees have colorful leaves in the fall. _______

2. I might fall if I run too fast down the hill. _______

3. The last day of school will fall on a Friday. _______

Write a sentence for each meaning of the word fall .

4. ____

____

5. ____

____

6. ____

____

Correct the sentences.

1. That book is about a vet at the san diego zoo.

____

2. do you want to be a Zoo vet someday

____

Write the missing word.

3. _______________ as much as you can about animal science.

Teach   Learn   Learns

Write the missing word.

4. teacher : student :: vet : _______________

Correct the sentences.

1. A old man sitted on the bench and ate a apple.

____

2. His grandson sitted on the bensh, two.

____

Use because or and to make one sentence.

3. It was a sunny day. They enjoyed the sunshine.

____

Circle the root words .

4. power ful   following   likely   player

Correct the sentences.

1. i need some quietly time to work by myself.

____

2. I must finished my homewerk this afternoon.

____

Write the missing word.

3. I can't play now, ___________________ can you come back later?

     and   but   because

Circle the word that means come back .

4. I will be ready to play when you return.

Correct the sentences.

1. The third Sunday in july is national Ice Cream day.

____

2. long ago, ice cream was maid out of snow

____

Correct the run-on sentence . Write two shorter sentences.

3. I like vanilla ice cream the best we can have some later.

____

Circle the adverbs .

4. cold   later   drippy   sometimes

Read the adjectives and adverbs.

Adjectives	Adverbs
extra	never
sleepy	after
yellow	yet

Write the adjective or adverb that goes with each underlined word.

1. You will <u>feel</u> ________________ if you stay up too late.

2. Have you <u>done</u> your homework ________________?

3. I have ________________ <u>gone</u> to the zoo.

Write a sentence with each word you did not use.

extra

4. ____

____

yellow

5. ____

____

after

6. ____

____

Correct the sentences.

1. The cook yuses fresh food growed on the garden.

____

2. Today she is making squash soup salad and bread

____

Correct the **run-on sentence** **. Write two shorter sentences.**

3. I'm going to have a bowl of soup would you like one?

____

Circle the sentence that is **formal** **.**

4. Show up at 6:00.   Please arrive at 6:00.

Correct the sentences.

1. A group of monkeys is call a troop

____

2. spider monkeys have tail that can grip tree branchs.

____

Circle the **verb** **.**

3. Spider monkeys greet each other with a hug.

Use **commas** **to write one sentence.**

4. Spider monkeys eat nuts and fruits. They eat leaves and eggs.

____

Correct the sentences.

1. Farmer mike has a dog name pal.

____

2. Pals job is to herd the flock of sheeps.

____

Write the missing word.

3. Once Pal kept the sheep safe from a _________________ of wolves.

flock   crowd   pack

Circle the word that means happens daily .

4. everywhere   daydream   everyday

Correct the sentences.

1. We celebrated earth day on April 22.

____

2. A speaker told us about reuseing and recycleing

____

Use now or yet to rewrite the sentence.

3. We recycle cans, plastic, and paper.

____

Circle the word that means use something again .

4. usable   reuse   unused

Read the words and their definitions.

> **lay** *verb*
> to put down
>
> **lie** *verb*
> to rest with a flat body
>
> **layer** *noun*
> one thickness of something

Write the word that goes in each sentence.

1. Mom said to _______________ down for a nap.

2. Please _______________ the book on the table.

3. There was a _______________ of frosting on the cake.

Use each word to write a sentence.

4. ____

____

5. ____

____

6. ____

____

Correct the sentences.

1. What does you want to do on the fourth of july?

____

2. Lets learn about what happened on july 4 1776.

____

Write the missing word.

3. We can watch the parade march _________________ city hall.

　　　　　　　　　　before　　　during　　　toward

Circle the word that means a large number of people .

4. We should go early, because there will be a crowd.

Correct the sentences.

1. Dad got hisself a new camera at Erin's Camera Shop?

____

2. He took a picture at mom and I.

____

Rewrite the sentence using broadly and pink .

3. We were smiling in front of flowers.

____

Write the plural .

4. lady　　　　_________________

Correct the sentences.

1. A group of turtles is call a bale.

____

2. Some turtles can hid their head inside there shells.

____

Write the missing word.

3. A mother turtle _________________ eggs.

        lain   lays   lies

Circle the word that means **a trip** .

4. We saw a bale of turtles when we were on vacation last summer.

Correct the sentences.

1. On June 14 1777, the united states got a new flag.

____

2. June 14 was named national flag day in 1949.

____

Use **but** **to write one sentence.**

3. It's not a national holiday. Many people honor Flag Day.

____

Circle the word that means **show** .

4. On Flag Day, people display the flag and sing songs.

Read the nouns.

Singular	Plural
cactus	cacti
loaf	loaves
tomato	tomatoes

Write the noun that goes in each sentence.

1. We need to buy a _________________ of bread.

2. I will cut a _________________ to put in the salad.

3. Don't poke yourself on those two _________________.

Write a sentence using each plural noun.

4. ____

   ____

5. ____

   ____

6. ____

   ____

Correct the sentences.

1. sunflowers are plant that grow very quick.

____

2. They can grow 8 too 12 feet tall in six month's

____

Write the missing word.

3. The record for the _________________ sunflower is 27 feet.

    tall   taller   tallest

Write big or huge in the sentence.

4. That _________________ sunflower is as tall as our house!

Correct the sentences.

1. Baseball is won of the oldest sports played in america

____

2. Long ago, it was play like a english game called rounders.

____

Circle the word that means almost the same as new .

3. In 1845, the rules were changed to make modern baseball.

Write the opposite .

4. new   _________________

Correct the sentences.

1. Some scientists say that its healthy to smile

____

2. When you smile, it help your body brain and feelings.

____

Write the missing word.

3. Smiling can help _________________ talk to people.

        you   your   yourself

Circle the word that means almost the same as smile .

4. A happy grin can help everyone have a great day!

Correct the sentences.

1. last summer my dad and me build a treehouse.

____

2. We made a ladder four my frends and I to climb.

____

Circle the part of the sentence that tells what they do .

3. Up in the treehouse, we pretend that we are space travelers.

Write the missing word.

4. Mom brings tasty _________________ for us, too.

       snakes   snacks   snaks

Correct the journal. Rewrite it on the lines.

june 27 2015

Today we went to seal beach we had a great time I play in the sand. we eated sandwiches carrots and apples. a gull tuk my sandwich! Im glad we had extra food. dad and me play catch with a beach ball. we had alot of fun.

My Progress

Week	Number Correct Each Day					Skill I Did Well	Skill I Need to Practice
	1	2	3	4	5		
1							
2							
3							
4							
5							
6							
7							
8							
9							
10							
11							
12							
13							
14							
15							
16							
17							
18							

My Progress (cont.)

Week	Number Correct Each Day					Skill I Did Well	Skill I Need to Practice
	1	2	3	4	5		
19							
20							
21							
22							
23							
24							
25							
26							
27							
28							
29							
30							
31							
32							
33							
34							
35							
36							